IMAGES OF ENGLAND

BUDE AND DISTRICT
THE SECOND SELECTION

IMAGES OF ENGLAND

BUDE AND DISTRICT
THE SECOND SELECTION

ADRIAN ABBOTT

The wharf area of Bude in the 1960s. The railway track has been lifted but the premises of the Devon Trading Co., the Scout Hut and cobblers shop have yet to be demolished.

Frontispiece: The Millhouse at Coombe Valley, *c.* 1890.

First published in 2002 by Tempus Publishing

Reprinted in 2009 by
The History Press
The Mill, Brimscombe Port,
Stroud, Gloucestershire, GL5 2QG
www.thehistorypress.co.uk

Reprinted 2010

British Library Cataloguing in Publication Data.
A catalogue record for this book is available from the British Library.

ISBN 978 0 7524 2632 7

Typesetting and origination by Tempus Publishing.
Printed and bound in Great Britain by
Marston Book Services Limited, Oxford

Contents

Petvin's wine stores in 1906 was situated in Tapson's Terrace, which now forms part of the Strand, Bude.

Introduction

This book is a personal choice of pictures taken largely from my own collection of postcards. These have been augmented with cards and photographs kindly loaned by friends.

The book does not set out to teach the history of the area but to glimpse the past, jog memories and awaken a desire to further explore this rural part of Cornwall.

Early pictures were taken by photographers such as Thorn, Knight, Broad, Dempster and Calvert. From their pictures come poignant images recording an era of change. However it is the personal snaps with named groups of local families that bring the collection to life, evoking memories for both residents and visitors.

Bude, for years secondary in importance to Stratton, is now the larger town and is still growing at a rapid rate. With expansion has come change and transformation. The Railway Station, Grammar School and Picture House have all sadly gone, along with the vibrant shipping trade, however new structures abound including a newly furbished comprehensive school, sports hall, bowling alley, swimming pool and new houses and shops.

Agriculture, the backbone of the regions economy, has had to adjust considerably to survive modern pressures. The tourist industry is constantly endeavouring to attract visitors. Despite this the landscape and beauty of the area remains for all to see and enjoy.

The images I have chosen for this book are mainly from the early to middle years of the twentieth century – an age of steam trains and sailing ships, a time when tradesmen delivered all sorts of supplies to your door and the motor car was for the lucky few. Nostalgic rural scenes, local and historical events are included to record life in our 'recent past'.

Acknowledgements

I am very grateful to all the local people that have given me such encouragement in the compilation of this book, and I hope the end product does justice to your contributions. Particular thanks must go to the following people who have helped with information, or provided pictures from family albums:

Mary Jury, Gerry Pennington, Trevor Furse, Richard and Mary Wickett, Fred Jeffery, Bryan Stamp, Bert and Anne Tape, Peter Truscott, Anne Cave, John Kinver, Margaret Trewin, Francis Walkey, Julie Shepherd, Heather Burden, Brenda Crocker-White, Mike Smith, Dave Hosking, Ken Colwill and Carol Smith.

Also thanks to the *St Gennys Gazette* and St Hilarys Residential Home. I must also mention the postcard dealers around the country with whom I have traded for many years, notably Christine Booth, June Puttick, Peter Bray, Peter Andrews and Peter Johnson.

Finally thanks to my wife, Jill, who unwittingly began my collection by purchasing a bundle of Bude postcards in an antique shop in Camelford because she 'thought I may be interested!'

Foreword

Adrian Abbott is a Cornishman through and through, and comes from a highly respected Bude family. Three generations of the Abbott family have been associated with the Railway in Bude, and Adrian's love of Cornwall, particularly north Cornwall, is very dear to his heart. A keen deltiologist, he has over the years collected thousands of postcards and photographs of the area and his book depicts the most northerly parishes of Cornwall, stretching from Marsland Mouth in the parish of Morwenstow on the Devon-Cornwall border, down to the parish of St Gennys. Roughly in the centre lie Bude and Stratton, whilst inland we look towards Week St Mary and North Tamerton. All aspects of life in these areas are featured in this fascinating book, many pictures are collector's items and have never been published before. As we browse through this superb collection, featuring over 240 postcards and photographs, we can appreciate the tremendous amount of time Adrian has put into compiling *Bude and District: The Second Selection*.

It is with thanks to Adrian that residents, visitors and those who have fond memories of this lovely part of Cornwall, can now sit back and take a nostalgic trip down memory lane, which I know you are going to enjoy.

Thank you also, Adrian, for giving me the privilege to write the foreword of this unique book, and in true Cornish tradition, you have certainly done a 'proper job'.

Ray Shaddick, BBC Radio Cornwall.

One

Business and Trade

In the early 1900s Bude's shopping centre is beginning to take shape. These shops along the Strand were among the first retail premises. The Bude Hotel, at the junction with Belle Vue, was demolished in 1905 to make way for Lloyds Bank. The fence bordering the river was made from wires salvaged from the wreck of the *Bencoolen* in 1862. It was still there almost one hundred years later.

Stratton and Bude have had a 'parent and child' relationship over the centuries. The history of Stratton and its surrounding villages goes back to Anglo-Saxon times and beyond with Stratton being very much the leading player. Bude, or 'Bewd', adjacent to 'Bede's Haven – the Haven of the 'Holy men' who lit a warning lamp on Chapel Rock at the end of the present day Breakwater – was for many years the Port for Stratton, a mere collection of cottages, sailors inns and warehouses. In addition there was a vast stretch of sand at low tide where ships could be beached and their cargoes unloaded. With the coming of the Bude Canal in 1820 and the Railway in 1898 this relationship was to change. Bude grew up to become the 'resort' we know today whilst Stratton gradually retired gracefully.

Outside the Parish Hall, Bude, during the First World War, is Charlie Heard and Bill Wonnacott delivering milk from Wonnacott's dairy at Rodds Bridge.

Maynard's shop, known as the London House, on the Strand at Bude in 1911. This was later to become the local Conservative Club.

Keat's shop in Princes Street, Bude, following alterations in 1908. The street was named after the four sons of Queen Victoria.

Sampson's staff pictured with their new delivery van at the rear of the bakery in Lansdowne Road, Bude, in 1911.

The Strand, Bude.

This imposing shop frontage belonged to Stationer and Chemist G. Wise in 1940. It was situated in the heart of Bude's commercial district opposite the main bus stop.

In 1938 Springfield House was at the top of Belle Vue. After demolition it was rebuilt by F.J. Edwards and became the 'Emporium'. In later years this changed to the Co-op, and then the Merchantman.

Gerald Davey, delivery driver for Kinver & Kinver, bakers of Stratton and Holsworthy, seen here with his van around 1910.

Flexbury Supply Stores was located in Summerleaze Avenue. As Prettijohn's grocery store it traded until the 1960s. The hardware shop on the right became the Green Tub Café. Both premises have now been redeveloped as residential accommodation.

Employees of Frederick Cann, Master Builder, engaged on the construction of Bude Railway Station in 1898. His two sons, Archie and Fred, continued the family business as Cann Bros.

Archie Abbott delivering meat in the Flexbury area of Bude in 1917. He was an employee of E. Tucker, a butcher in Belle Vue. Shortly after this picture was taken he was called up for Military service in France. Following the Armistice he joined the London & South Western Railway at Bude, which he served until his death in 1961.

The old brewery buildings at Poundstock. Brewing ended at the outbreak of the First World War in 1914 when the German owners were interned.

THE NORTH CORNWALL BREWERY
——And Aerated Water Factory,——
POUNDSTOCK, BUDE.

THE position of the Brewery and Factory on the summit of a hill ensures a **Perfectly Pure Water Supply.** The quality of the water is vouched for by one of the leading analysts of the day (Lawrence Briant, Esq., F.C.S., F.R.M.S., etc., Consulting Analyst to Messrs. Bass, Allsopp, Guinness, etc.).

**THE BEST MALT AND HOPS ONLY ARE USED,
. . consequently satisfaction is guaranteed . .**

The Buildings have been recently erected, and are therefore thoroughly up to date, and fitted with best modern appliances. Our vans supply the whole of the district, and visitors and residents are invited to give our products a trial.
AGENTS: Bottled Beers and Stouts—PETVIN & CO., Bude; Casks—PETHERICK & CO., Bude Haven.

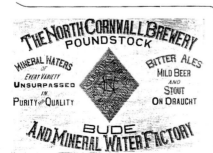

Aerated Waters
at all the leading Grocers and Chemists.

All the principal Hotels of the District supplied.

HOME-BREWED GINGER BEER
A SPECIALITY.

Kindly note our name on our special Diamond-shaped Labels,

SLAUGHTER & DOMINY.

An advertisement dated 1906 for the brewery products.

Barrett's furniture shop in Queen Street, Bude. The business began in 1880 and traded through four generations of the same family before finally closing in 2001.

Following completion of the Congregational Church in 1935, employees of the builder Messrs. Pethick Bros. gather to commemorate the moment. This firm, which acted for the local Grenville and Thynne Estates, was responsible for the construction of many of Bude's streets in the early part of the twentieth century. From left to right, front row: Frankie Lyle, Kim Bolt, Cecil Balsdon, Harry Brimacombe, Arthur Pethick, Harry Hallett, Alf Barrett, Jam Short, -?-, -?-. Kneeling: Curley Joliffe, Jack Kerridge, George Vanstone. Middle row: Bob Yeo, Bill Luxton, Dick Penfound, Jan Rogers (Snr), Tom Bassett, ? Jones, -?-, Bill Cornish, Duggie Pearse, Sam Fry, Freddie Wiltshire, Reg Grills, Sid Short, Alf Worth, -?-, -?-, George Staddon. Back row: Harold Gratton, Cyril Colwill, Bill Davey, ? Cann, ? Brown, Jack Bennett, Bill Jones, Arthur Weston, Arthur Ditchburn, Jan Rogers (Jnr), Gennie Gilbert, Ern Gilbert, Harold Inch, Bill Ford.

In 1909 Westlakes shop in Marhamchurch was not only the village Post Office but also Draper and Grocer.

Pictured outside the Bullers Arms, Marhamchurch, in 1912, are the landlady Mrs Gloyn and her daughter.

Trewin's all-purpose store in Kilkhampton at the turn of the twentieth century.

'Royal Daylight' Petroleum.

PRESENT MARKET PRICES.

From 4 to 10 Gallon lots........................per gallon.

Royal Daylight per Barrel...................................

Russian Rocklight for Engines per Barrel..............

Barrels or Drums refilled from Store Tank.

Barrels charged 1d. per gallon if not returned.

☞ Special Line in Smokeless Cartridges. ☜

RABBIT TRAPS AND SNARING WIRES.

F. TREWIN, Ironmonger and
Ammunition Dealer,

KILKHAMPTON.

A postcard used to advertise the current prices of Mr Trewin's petrol. A far cry from the self-service pumps of today.

65 S. Gennys Post Office

Interestingly, St Gennys Post Office is not in St Gennys but in Jacobstow, the parish boundary runs along the main road. There is a Post Office at Higher Crackington which is in St Gennys parish.

Two local postmen on their rounds. Above is Bryant Jewell at Crackington Haven in 1929, and on the right is Jack Hambly at Coombe Valley in 1931.

Jacobstow in the early twentieth century. The sign reads, 'Frederick Piper, Draper, Grocer and Tea dealer, Licensed to sell Tobacco and Snuff'.

A group of tradesmen and estate workers pause for the camera during work at Ogbeare Hall, North Tamerton, in the early 1900s. Many are holding the tools of their trade.

The commercial centre of Stratton, known as Bank corner, in the 1930s. Stratton was at one time the major town in the area with its banks, court, businesses and police station. Its importance declined as Bude grew, largely due to the opening of the railway and the expansion of the holiday trade.

Kinver & Kinver's bakery shop in Fore Street, Stratton, around 1930. Standing in front is Garfield Jennings, Richard Kinver who started the business in 1900, and a young John Kinver.

Seen here is the work force employed at New Road Quarry, Tiscott between Stratton and Kilkhampton during the Second World War, when stone was quarried for use on the roads. Among those posing for the photograph are George Vinnicombe, Arthur Braund, Charles Jenkins, Ned Littlejohn, Jack White, Titus Brimacombe, Fred Dymond, Monty Wilson, Curly Bird, Harry Gittens, Harry Paddon, Dick Fanson, Bill Thomas, Sam Coombe, Alfred Burrows, Bill Paddon, Dick Venner, Charles Bailey, Thomas Heard, Harold Lane, Bill Mills, Arthur J. Braund, Stanley Blackmoor and Bill Thorn.

Tape's covered wagon in 1904 collecting grain from the surrounding farms for milling at Coombe Mill, five miles north of Bude. The driver is Tommy Hambly of Stibb.

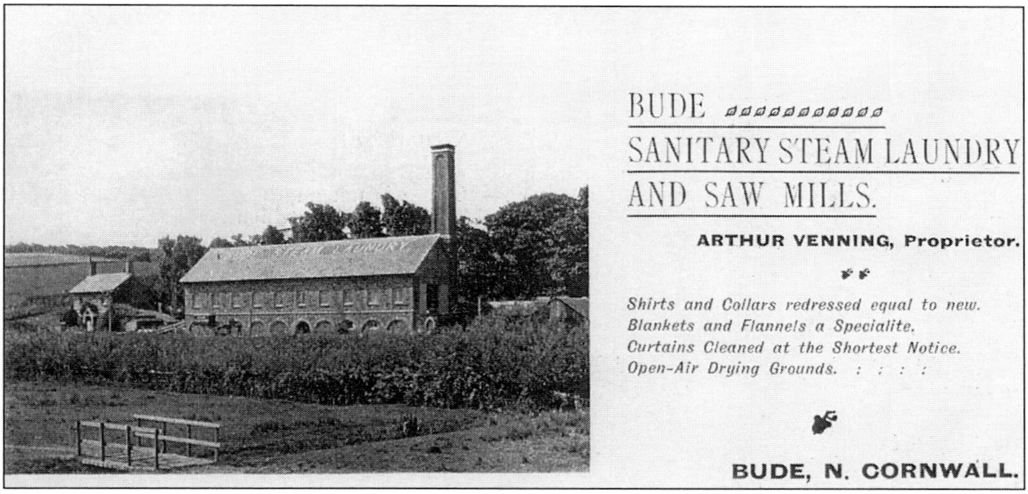
BUDE
SANITARY STEAM LAUNDRY
AND SAW MILLS.
ARTHUR VENNING, Proprietor.
Shirts and Collars redressed equal to new.
Blankets and Flannels a Specialite.
Curtains Cleaned at the Shortest Notice.
Open-Air Drying Grounds. : : : :
BUDE, N. CORNWALL.

The Bude Sanitary Steam Laundry situated beside the canal, around 1906. It was built around 1840 as a sawmill to supply timber for Stapleton's Shipyard close by. The chimney has gone but the building has been tastefully redeveloped for residential use. The occupants have fine views over the canal towards Bude's nature reserve.

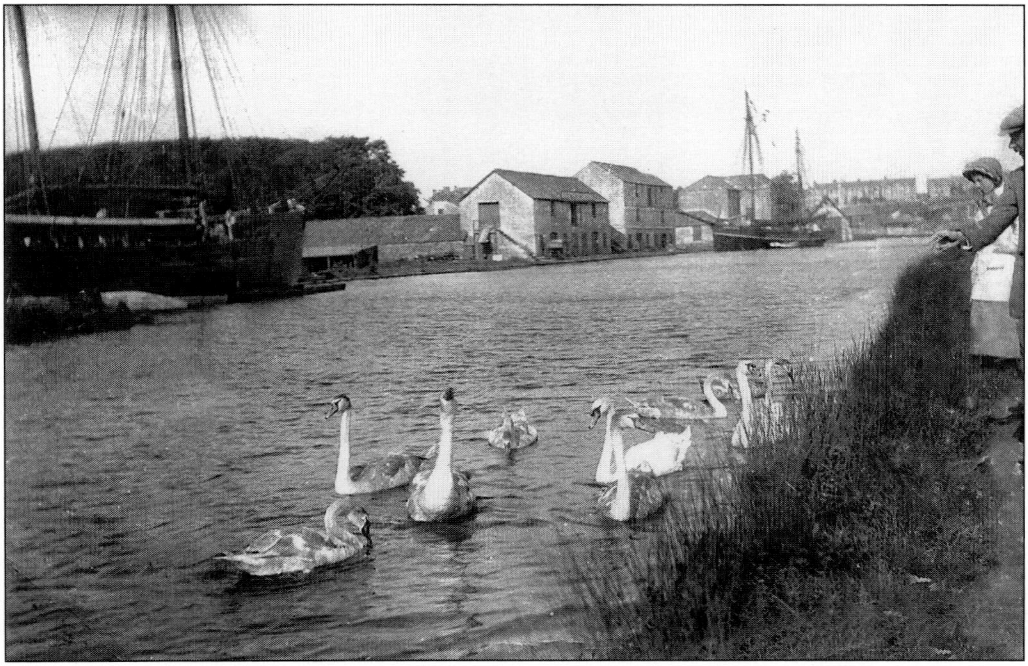

At the beginning of the 1900s Bude possessed its own shipbuilding and repair yard situated in the upper basin of the canal. Ships from Stapleton's yard, seen here on the left, would be launched sideways before passing through Falcon swingbridge and on to the sea lock. In the background another vessel is unloading at Pethericks wharf.

The New Inn at Kilkhampton, *c.* 1920. Standing outside are the owners, the Trewin family: Alfred (Senior), Alfred (Junior), Ellen Louise and Barbara. To the right, outside the bootmakers shop is Vivian Trewin.

Week St Mary in the early part of the century. Higgins cobblers and general merchandise shop.

Queen Street, Bude, named after Queen Victoria and completed in 1900.

Spencer Colwill delivering dairy produce to the Morwenstow area in the 1930s.

The wheelwrights shop belonging to N. Treleaven in Stratton, *c.* 1880.

In the late 1880s, Heard's family grocers shop stood at the western end of the Crescent, Bude. It advertises co-operative prices! This site is now occupied by the Crescent Post Office. In the centre of the row of houses is the double-fronted shop belonging to Burrows, a painter, plumber and furniture maker.

Two

Transport and Travel

A 'Morwenna Grey' charabanc operated by Edwards garage in Morwenna Terrace, Bude.

Stratton was connected to the outside world by a reasonable 'Coach Road' to Exeter. In addition there were roads both to the North – Bideford, the South – Camelford, and inland to Launceston. Stagecoaches made their final journeys in the 1920s as the motor car took over the roads. The shipping trade greatly increased with the building of the Bude Canal and Sea locks in the 1820s. It was the coming of the London & South Western Railway in 1898 which finally made Bude one of the leading 'seaside resorts' of the South West.

Today it is almost impossible to imagine this scene from 1940. The station buildings and gas works have disappeared, replaced by housing. Stratton Road leads off to the left.

September 1958. A Drummond T9 30715 backs onto coaches at Bude's platform No. 2. We see The Crescent and Westcliffe Hotel to the left beyond the station allotments.

Some of the staff at Bude railway station just after the war. From left to right: Jim Baker, Dorothy Brown, Bill Burridge, Betty Martin, Fred Partridge, Dan Stacey, Vernon Cloke, Archie Abbott, Ted Holwill.

Three tickets sold on the last day of service at Bude in 1966, the child's 2nd single to Whitstone and Bridgerule being the very last ticket ever issued.

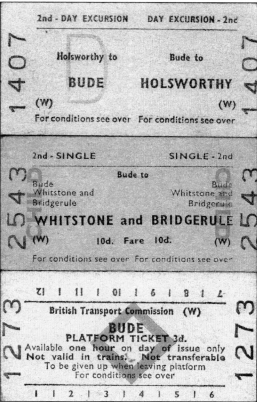

A goods train passes the now unused lock gates near Rodds Bridge in 1907. The railway contributed towards the demise of the canal trade, but whilst the canal remains today there is little to remind us of the railway. Recent regeneration of the canal has seen the lock gates returned to working order.

Removing the boiler from the *Arran Monarch* in 1962. This was the last ship-to-rail transfer at Bude.

A fine picture of small coastal trading vessels waiting to pass through the lock gates. Nearest the camera is the ill-fated *President Garfield* destined to be wrecked off Summerleaze in March 1906.

Taking advantage of the high tide and calm sea, this is one of many craft to use Bude around 1920.

The SS *Woodbridge*, which ran aground at Northcott Mouth on 4 April 1915. She was refloated successfully a few days later.

An earlier casualty at Northcott Mouth was the steam trawler *Scotia* in May 1909.

Heavy snow in 1955 brought this bus to an unscheduled stop outside Kilkhampton.

Also in 1955, Golf House Hill, Bude, is rendered impassable until the Council workmen have completed their task.

Three Leyland buses await their passengers on the Strand at Bude. This area continues to be the main bus stop for the town.

Henry 'Granfer' Smith at Poundstock in 1938 with his tricycle.

Heavy traffic through Kilkhampton in the early 1900s! Brendon's coaches continued to run until well into the 1920s with a regular service to Clovelly and Bideford. It must be summertime judging by the heavy foliage on the trees in the churchyard.

This picture is taken from almost exactly the same spot as the previous one but over forty years later. It shows a selection of cars outside the London Inn during the Second World War. Note the whitened edges to the running boards and mudguards, a safety measure during the wartime blackout.

Reg Burden on his Raleigh motorcycle, *c.* 1940. He was a well-known local figure and an officer in the Home Guard during the war. He died in 2001.

Eddie Sandercock driving a jingle past the Coombe Barton in Crackington Haven, *c.* 1915.

Members of the Fry family of Bristol, famous for their chocolates, photographed outside
Hartland House in Bude in 1910, which later became the Hartland Hotel.

Not really ideal for the narrow country lanes – a Southern National double-decker bus at
Marhamchurch in 1958. The views of the countryside from the top deck must have made it an
interesting journey.

Stratton Sunday School prepare to set off for an outing in the early 1920s under the watchful eye of Revd Cyril Leslie Jones. Their destination was most probably Widemouth Bay, where games were played on the beach and refreshments taken in the Widemouth Tea Rooms.

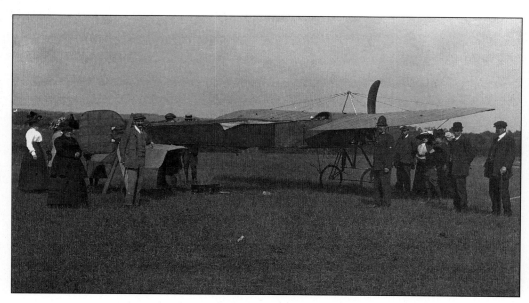

Henri Salmet landed the *Daily Mail* aeroplane at Bude in 1912, in the area of Broadclose, providing many of Bude's residents with their first glimpse of an aircraft.

Three

Duty and Religion

Stratton Hospital is believed to be the second oldest cottage hospital in Britain, and continues to provide a valuable service to a widely scattered and isolated community. The original hospital building – 'Supported by voluntary contributions' – was opened in 1866.

This chapter ranges over the whole concept of 'Local Duty' to the Community. Bude and district did its duty in both World Wars, nursing wounded soldiers in the First and providing one of the vital anti aircraft practice camps in the Second. The sea is always with us and with it came the Lifeboat and Coastguard services. Stratton Church of St Andrew led the way of religion since Saxon times along with many other churches in the area. Since the nineteenth century 'Methodism' and other breakaway sects have been strong in Cornwall. The many chapels built are well represented here.

Stratton Cottage Hospital. By the time this card was posted in 1909 a small extension had been added.

1935, and the hospital had continued to grow, with a further extension opened.

With the considerable assistance of the League of Friends, this card shows that in 1958 the hospital boasted a male and female ward, operating theatre and staff quarters.

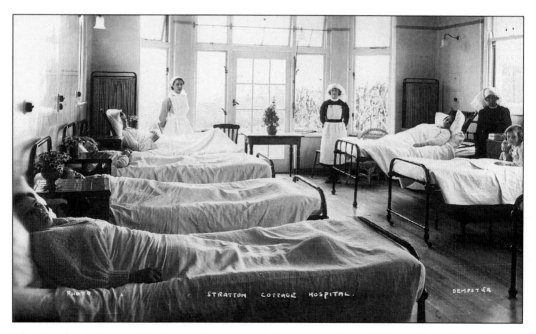

The female ward in 1958. The staff are, from left to right: Nurse Nolan, Sister Glanfield and Matron Brown.

Margaret Brown, Matron 1954-1958.

Stratton hospital staff 'on parade' to mark the opening of the new casualty department in 1964.
From left to right, back row: Marjorie Taylor (night sister), May Helson (SEN), Moira Hallett and
Marilyn Grills (auxilliaries), Horace Lyle (male attendant), ? Pooley (theatre sister), Rose Thompson
(night sister), June Middleton and Lorna Cobbledick (auxilliaries), Mary Jury (part-time sister),
Amy Glandfield (ward sister). Front row: Dr Blood (Bude/Stratton), Dr Brown (Holsworthy), Dr
Betts (Bradworthy), Dr Byrne (Bude/Stratton), Mrs Barrett (matron), Dr Craddock (Holsworthy),
Dr Pearson (Holsworthy), Dr Corser (Bude/Stratton) and Dr Munks (Bude/Stratton).

Troops paraded for inspection, 1908. The location is believed to be Maer Down, Bude.

Marhamchurch, 4 May 1938. The funeral with full military honours for Sergeant-Major William Paddon of the Duke of Cornwall's Light Infantry.

Church Parade. Bude. 24. May 14. *S. Thorn. photo*

A church parade held on Efford Down, Bude, to mark Empire Day, 24 May 1914. Within weeks these troops would be at war.

Horses for the War, *Bude,* *Aug. 5th. 1914.* *Broad photo.*

Not only men but horses were needed for the battlefields of France. A collection is taking place in Lansdown Road. In the background is the premises of N.J. Hawking, shipping agent, now N.E. Truscott's hardware shop.

The Home Guard practising the use of a Lewis machine gun on Summerleaze Downs overlooking Crooklets beach, during the Second World War.

During the Second World War coastal defences were prepared at all possible invasion beaches. At Northcott Mouth the concrete Dragons Teeth are clearly visible and many remained until long after the war had ended.

The Crackington and St Gennys platoons of the Home Guard on parade at the Haven. In the background are well-tended vegetable gardens helping the war effort.

Cleave Camp, high on the cliffs at Morwenstow, began operational duties in 1939. Known as RAF Cleave, it was to provide anti-aircraft gunnery training for Territorial Army units. It continued to perform this role into the mid 1950s.

A flight of Westland Wallace aircraft stationed at RAF Cleave at the beginning of the Second World War. They towed the targets for the army's gunners at the practice camp.

Red Cross nurses practising their skills on the troops at Cleave Camp.

On a rainy day in 1939. The unusual sight of a 4.5' anti-aircraft gun standing in the square at Kilkhampton awaiting transport to Cleave Camp.

A letter from W.H. Smith & Son who ran the bookstall on the railway station at Bude.

Bude's Rocket Brigade Volunteers and Coastguards rescuing the crew of *Crystal Spring* using the rocket apparatus and breeches buoy. August 1904.

Left: The RNLI has always relied on contributions and the work of volunteer collectors. Seen here in Flexbury Park Road around 1930 is Lily Mason with her tray of 'flags'. *Right*: The Bude Coastguard team practising on the cliffs beneath the storm tower using a cliff ladder in 1920.

Bude lifeboat having been brought ashore at Widemouth, *c.* 1905.

The RNLB *Princess Mary*, seen here in 1936 celebrating lifeboat day at Bude, was a 61ft Barnett type lifeboat built in 1929. She served at Padstow until 1952 and is credited with saving a total of forty-eight lives. Sold out of service for £1,000 to C. Harcourt-Smith of London, she became the twin screw motor yacht *Aries R*, and in 1954 became the first motor boat to cross the Atlantic both ways without the assistance of sails, reaching New York in thirty-three days and returning in twenty-three.

Bude lifeboat in the canal basin alongside the local ketch *Jessie, c.* 1900. In 1904 the *Jessie* became stranded in the canal when a wave broke the lock gates and drained the canal. Behind her the tall stone building is Rocket House, which housed the equipment used by the Rocket Brigade Volunteers.

The annual ceremony of 'Blessing the Sea' takes place at the breakwater. Officiating here is the Revd C. Atkin, Vicar of Bude 1932-1944.

11 November 1922, Bude unveiled its war memorial. Many of the surnames inscribed thereon appear throughout Bude's history.

Very few villages escaped loss during the First World War. *Left*: Stratton commemorates its fallen with this memorial column, unveiled on 11 November 1920. *Right*: It is appropriate that the typical inland Cornish village of Week St Mary should adopt the 'Cross of Cornwall' as its memorial.

In memory of an even earlier conflict, this structure marks the site of the battle of Stamford Hill, near Stratton, in 1643. It resulted in a victory for the smaller Cornish army, under Sir Bevil Grenville, over the Parliamentarian forces.

April 1905. The opening of Flexbury Park Methodist church, Bude, by J.B. Butler Esq. It is one of very few Methodist churches to have a spire. Many of the interior fittings such as the pulpit and pews were made from pitch pine salvaged from a wreck near Millook, to the south of Widemouth.

The Vicarage, Ebbingford Manor. At one time this was a manor house belonging to the Arundel family. In 1943 it became the Headquarters of one of the American army units stationed locally whilst training for D-Day.

Left: St. Michael and all Angels church, *c.* 1910. Built in 1835 by Sir Thomas Acland as a chapel of ease, it became the parish church of Bude in 1848. *Right*: a photograph of the fine carved rood screen and pulpit in Kilkhampton church, taken in 1909.

St Martins Congregational church in Killerton Road, Bude, opened in 1935.

The ivy-covered Norman tower of the church of St Marwenne at Marhamchurch. She was a daughter of the Welsh king Brychan who travelled to Cornwall in the fifth century.

St James Day parade at Kilkhampton in 1909.

No mention of religion in North Cornwall can overlook the Revd Robert Stephen Hawker of Morwenstow. He would often go to the cliffs to meditate, overlooking the Atlantic Ocean in his hut constructed of driftwood. It must be one of the smallest National Trust properties in Britain.

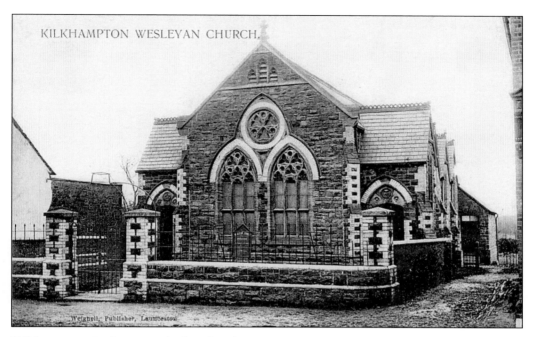

Kilkhampton Wesleyan Methodist church, *c.* 1910.

The old chapel in the grounds of Reeds at Poughill photographed at the turn of the twentieth century.

The impressive lych-gate at the entrance to Kilkhampton church.

The small church of St Peter at Stibb, between Poughill and Kilkhampton, decorated for harvest festival. It has now been converted into a private dwelling.

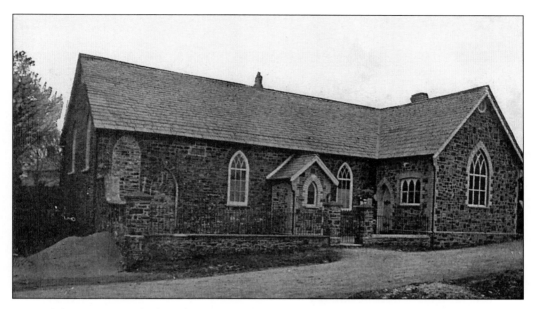

One of the many small chapels to serve the rural community is this one at Eastcott near Morwenstow, c. 1920. Like so many others, it has been converted for private use. The last service held here was for Harvest Festival on 9 October 1977.

The interior of Eastcott chapel, just prior to its closure.

Left: Revd W. Swinerton, vicar of Poundstock, in 1909. *Right*: Revd John Allsopp, Vicar of Jacobstow, in the 1930s.

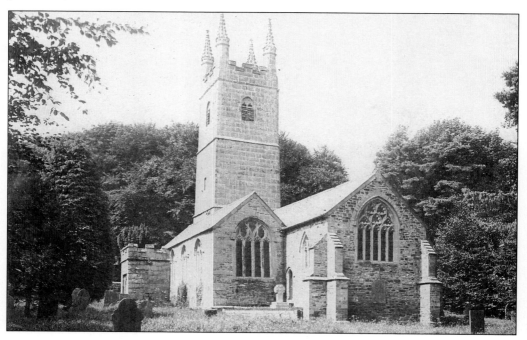

St James church, Jacobstow.

The distinctive tower roof of St Gennys church only survived two winters before the Norman pattern tower was rebuilt in 1910.

Left: Sporting one of the tallest towers in the area, built in 1543 and visible from the coast several miles away, is Week St Mary church. This picture dates from the 1920s. *Right*: dating from the early Norman period, this double cable font at Launcells church was most probably made by Saxon craftsmen. The list of vicars for this church dates back to 1261. In the churchyard is buried the inventor Sir Goldsworthy Gurney.

St Andrews church, Stratton, *c.* 1900. There is believed to have been a church on this site since Saxon times. Norman relics were found during renovations in the nineteenth century.

Stratton's new peal of bells, dedicated on St Andrews day 30 November 1911. The original eight bell peal dates from 1558.

Four

Town and Country

An early litho photographic view of Bude, in the area of The Crescent.

This delightful set of photographs provide a wonderful contrast between Bude and Stratton, and the adjacent villages with the surrounding countryside. It gives a picture of a growing 'seaside resort' with its new set of 'terraces' alongside a countryside which had not changed for centuries. Here are all the old farming customs – sheep dipping, threshing, ploughing, milking, feeding the hens, and so on. It all seems so timeless and in great contrast to the rush of today.

Now called The Crescent, it was known in the early years by a number of different names, notably Frying Pan Row, South Terrace and Shalder Terrace. Lord Tennyson, the Victorian Poet Laureate, spent some time at no. 12 during 1848 whilst recovering from a broken leg.

Sunblinds are very much in evidence in Morwenna Terrace during a fine day in the 1920s. This terrace was built in 1888.

One of the oldest streets in Bude is King Street. Most of the properties remain in the ownership of the Blanchminster Charity. Seen here decorated for Armistice Day, 1945.

Downs View, part of the Flexbury Estate, developed by Pethick Bros. between 1901-1910. Many of these fine large properties soon became guest houses catering for the holiday makers.

Looking inland from Penkenna Point, St Gennys, we see a patchwork of fields so typical of the region in the 1920s prior to development.

This postcard of St Catherines, Crackington Haven, c. 1912, includes the grounded railway carriage, used as additional accommodation. As Otterham station was five miles away, it would have been quite a feat by teams of horses to transport it to this final destination.

The old terrace of cottages in Sanctuary Lane, Stratton, at the end of the nineteenth century.

This aerial photograph of Millook, taken in the 1930s, clearly shows the steep slopes and hairpin bends which have caught out many unwary drivers.

Rural tranquility in the 1950s. Rosecare Green near Crackington was not always this peaceful, for many years it was the venue for Cornish Wrestling Tournaments.

The old cottages at Ludon farm, Crackington Haven, *c.* 1905.

Tresparrett Posts in the 1930s, on the road to Boscastle. The building on the left was once the Red Lion public house.

Set in a deeply wooded valley stands the hamlet of New Mills in the parish of Poundstock, seen here in the 1940s.

TO
OILMEN, IRONMONGERS,
AND OTHERS.

The STRATTON AND BUDE URBAN DISTRICT COUNCIL are desirous of obtaining TENDERS for Lighting the Street Lamps in Stratton and Bude, under the following conditions :

1. The lighting to commence on the 12th August in this year, and to continue until the 30th of April next year inclusive.

2. On 7 nights of full, bright, moonlight in each month, the Contractor to be exempted from lighting, subject however to the discretion of the Council, who reserve the right to require the Contractor to light on either of the 7 nights should they think it expedient; in which case the Contractor to be paid for so lighting at per night in proportion to his Tender sum.

3. The Person tendering will be required to supply Royal Day-light Petroleum Oil, to renew Chimneys and Wicks, and to render the same in sound condition at the completion of his contract.

4. The Lamps to be lit each night at the commencement of dusk, and to be kept, while burning, turned up to their full candle power, to the satisfaction of the Council's Surveyor, and not to be extinguished before 10.30 o'clock p.m.

5. There are 33 Lamps to be lit for Stratton, and 63 for Bude.

6. Separate Tenders to be sent in for lighting Stratton and Bude.

7. No contractor to be allowed to sub-let his contract to another person.

Tenders, endorsed "Tenders for Lighting," to be sent in addressed to me not later than 4 o'clock on Friday the 9th August next.

The Council will not undertake to accept the Lowest or any Tender.

G. G. H. GURNEY,
Clerk to the Stratton & Bude Urban District Council.

Council Offices, Bude, 29th July, 1907.

PERRY BOLT, ELECTRIC MACHINE PRINTER, BUDE AND STRATTON.

Notice of tender for the street lighting in Bude and Stratton in 1907.

Upper Lynstone farm in the 1920s. The upturned, part boat, shelter remained a landmark for people entering Bude by the coast road from Widemouth for many years.

Bude Fair was traditionally held each September and drew crowds from far and wide to the many stalls along the Strand and nearby streets.

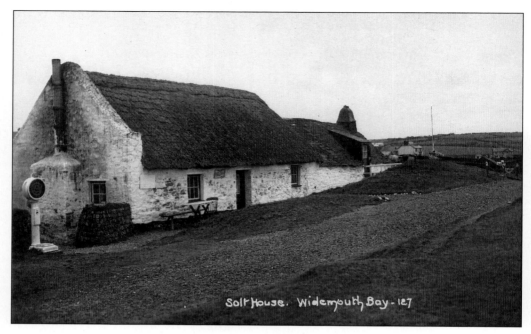

The Salt House, Widemouth Bay, *c.* 1920. It is believed by many to be the oldest surviving inhabited dwelling in this area.

Thatched roofs are much in evidence in the hamlet of Woodford, near Morwenstow.

Widemouth Bay in the 1930s. In the background can be seen the start of residential development.

Ogbeare Hall, with its fine gardens, is on the outskirts of North Tamerton. In recent times it became a residential home for the elderly.

Jack and Harry Pearse take a rest after negotiating the hill out of Millook. In the background is the panoramic view of Bude Bay.

Millook Ford at the beginning of the twentieth century.

A view of Week St Mary from the church tower in 1910.

Week St Mary became famous through the exploits of Thomasine Bonaventure who found fame and fortune in London. In 1499 her third husband, Sir John Percivall, became Lord Mayor. She never forgot her links to the village and this picture is of the old 'Grammerscole' which she founded.

Halfway along the road from Bude to Launceston stands the village of Whitstone.

No indication of the traffic problems which were to come to Poughill in later years when this picture was taken, *c.* 1910.

The old cottages at Northcott Mouth in the late 1800s.

Woolley, close to the Devon border, stands near to an ancient burial mound which was last excavated in 1968 to allow for realignment of the A39. The hamlet has changed little since this picture was taken in the mid 1930s. The building on the right housed Down's bakery.

Spicers Lane in Stratton, one of the narrow back lanes of this quaint old village.

These children take a break to pose for the camera outside Leat Cottages in Stratton around 1909. A number of these cottages date from the seventeenth century.

Parking presents no problem in Kilkhampton in 1910.

The old thatched blacksmith's premises at North Tamerton, believed to be in the late 1920s.

Working the sawmill at Coombe Valley, near Bude, in 1932. Above are Jack Jones, Francis Moore and Claude Tape, and on the right Herbert and Claude Tape.

The sawmill trolley for propelling long lengths of timber towards the saw blade.

Sheep dipping by King William Bridge at Coombe in 1933.

A threshing team from Hamblys of Whitstone working at Trewint farm, Poundstock, in the 1930s. Teams such as this would travel from farm to farm during the harvest season.

Jack Jeffrey and Dick Short with a Marshall traction engine at Chapel Farm, Morwenstow, in 1940. This machine was unique in that it was built to the specifications of its original owner, a Mr Goddard of Dorset. It was fitted with extra wide wheels and Pickering governors.

Left: Several years earlier than the previous picture, a much younger Jack Jeffrey is shown here with his Marshall 6hp two shaft traction engine. Not only was this a very rare model, but it was the first engine to appear in North Cornwall in the early 1900s. *Right:* Sand being collected from Black Rock beach at Widemouth for spreading on the fields. Being rich in minerals it provided a cheap form of fertilizer. Visible in the background is Black Rock which gives its name to the beach.

A steam-driven threshing machine working at Chapel Farm, Morwenstow.

Stratton market in 1928. George Brendon and Alfred Petherick, two well-known local businessmen, admiring the stock.

The art of thatching the ricks. It is a skill which has all but disappeared nowadays, and has no place in modern farming.

Ploughing a lonely furrow. No longer considered cost effective, this scene from the 1930s can now only be found at agricultural fairs and competitions.

Time for a short back and sides in the farmyard. Fred Hicks is the barber, William Henry Furse Senior is the customer, and Henry Smith awaits his turn. Bob the sheepdog takes a nap in the sun.

The market at Wainhouse Corner in 1938. Small weekly markets such as this were a cornerstone of rural life, both as a social gathering and where business was conducted.

Milking time.

Taking a break during a hard day's work.

Cleaning and polishing the tack. On a busy farm everyone had their chores to do.

Winifred Furse is feeding the hens.

Left: William Henry Furse stops for a drink from the pump at Dimma, Poundstock, on the way home from Sunday school. *Right*: Picking the beans. The cottage garden provided food for the table and a source of income – excess produce was sold at the local market.

Making the load. If not properly constructed it would soon fall off a moving wagon.

Five

Recreation and Education

Morwenstow band, seen here performing at Crosstown in the late 1800s.

The strength of any community is surely in its children. In this chapter we see the way they grew up and the schools they attended. It was a happy and healthy environment, although not without its hardships. Living in a growing seaside resort there was plenty going on with the seasons coming and going. Here are sea bathing, surfing, carnivals and even operas, with Cuckoo Fairs, maypoles and local village bands.

The recreation ground at Bude opened in 1924, catering for tennis, bowls and squash.

Bude Wesleyan Rovers Football Team First XI in the 1920/21 season. From left to right, back row: Frank Gregory, Chips Harris, Ken Marshall, Morris Cloke, Fred Chudley, ? Edwards. Front row: Fred Luxton, Silas Johns, Gordon Cann, Frank Cloke, Bonzo Pethick, Mr E.A. Wey (manager).

The open-air sea water swimming pool on Summerleaze Beach has been popular with holidaymakers and locals alike since its construction in 1930. The diving board did not last long however and would surely have fallen foul of safety regulations today!

Victory for one competitor in the greasy pole competition during Lifeboat Day celebrations in the 1930s.

Bude has always been famous for its surfing. Early body-boards were made of plywood and brightly painted. They could be hired from the nearby Council office at Crooklets Beach.

Bude must have one of the most exposed cricket pitches in the country. It has played host to the England Women's team, the Revd David Shepherd has scored a century here and it was mentioned by Brian Johnson during a Test Match commentary.

Suits and plus fours are the dress code for a visit to Crooklets Beach in 1917.

A fancy dress party held in the Martyn room at Crosstown, Morwenstow, in 1938. The room was presented to the parish by the Waddon-Martyn family of Tonnacombe Manor in the 1920s.

Celebration arches such as this one on the Strand at Bude were built to commemorate important events, such as the arrival of the railway in 1898.

Annual theatrical productions have been a feature in Bude for many years. Here in 1924 is the cast of the *Mikado* performed by Bude and Stratton Operatic Society.

Brigadier General James Ernest Vanrenen, 1865-1953, a resident of Summerleaze Crescent. The Vanrenen Cup is competed for annually at the local golf club.

A unique feature of Bude is the golf links which divides the town and is administered by the Bude and North Cornwall Golf Club. There was at one time a second course over Maer cliffs exclusively for patrons of the Falcon Hotel, but this no longer exists.

A class at Bude Primary School in 1920. From left to right, back row: Cyril Cloke, George Orange, Jack Worth, Tom Inch. Centre row: Clara White, Violet Jewell, Kath Wonnacott, Dorothy Marshall, Peggy Penfound, -?-, Mabel Haydon, -?-, Katie Spry, Kath Jeffrey, Win Dempster, Dorothy Cotton, Ivy Shepherd, Madge Harris. Seated: Brian Hockley, Harry Kinsman, George Brown, Jack Bickle, Duncan Johns.

With no playing field of their own, Bude Primary School held their annual open day in the castle grounds. Linda Vickery curtsies to Stephen Dell during the maypole dance in 1959. Rosemary Parsons looks on whilst supporting the pole.

The woodwork class at Stratton Secondary School in 1938.

A very attentive class at Stratton Secondary School in 1938, the year the school was opened.

Bude County School opened on 1 January 1909. It later became the Grammar School, one of the smallest in Britain. When the school amalgamated with Stratton Secondary to form Budehaven Comprehensive School in 1973, the site was flattened and St Hilarys Residential Home built in its place.

At Kilkhampton school in 1919, twenty-three pupils represented just ten families from the village. Seen here with the headmaster, Mr Williams and his staff are Marion, Wilfred, Winnie, Janie and Edith Axford; Sid, Lillian and Bill Thorn; John and Muriel Haywood; Ambrose, Ethel and Howard Metherall; Emma and Richard Wickett; Leslie and Ida Beer; Esther, Jane and Muriel Parkin; Lillian Brend; Marjorie Barrett and Ena Barnett.

Bude County School games pavilion erected by the boys at Broadclose, 1912.

Bude County School hockey XI in the 1913/14 season. At the back of the picture can be seen the main school building, the Headmaster's study was behind the bay window.

Kilkhampton Carnival Fairy Queen, Freda Trewin, poses with her attendants on her big day in 1958.

In 1908, a group collecting for the RNLI is seen outside Marshall's butchers shop in Princes Street, Bude. From left to right: Kathleen Burnard, Chrissie Welsh, Fred Box, Bertie Bewes, -?-, Alf Petherick, -?-.

A Christmas party arranged for evacuee children in the Parish Hall, Bude, during the Second World War.

In the centre of this group is Mrs Maynard on Misty as they prepare for the carnival in 1945. She ran the riding stables in Bude.

St Gennys continues the tradition of 'Beating the Bounds' of the parish to this day. Here parishioners pose at Rusey Cliff on the Southern most boundary in 1913.

Mr George Gaite rolls the first wood at Bude Bowling Club's opening day of the 1939 season.

Week St Mary band outside Burdenwell, *c.* 1920. This was an old dower house at one time and was the home of Sir Bevil Grenville's mother in the 1600s.

Ewart Gliddon, Stan Cowling and Charlie Cowling, three members of St Gennys band in 1920.

Jacobstow Church outing to Widemouth, Aug. 17th 1920

Churches were responsible for many of the social activities in the rural community. Here Jacobstow church members are pictured on an outing to Widemouth Bay in 1920.

Poughill Revel and Cuckoo Fair, c. 1932. These ladies (from left to right), Ada West, Blanche Benson, Violet Wroe, Dorothy Wroe and Sarah Watkins are at the parcel wrapping stall and all have a fine display of parasols. This event has been held on the first Thursday of every August since it was revived in 1927. Cuckoos refer to the ancient nickname for the men of Poughill parish.

The annual celebration of St James' Day at Kilkhampton in 1909 warranted the building of this arch, not possible with today's traffic, as this is the main A39 – now called the 'Atlantic Highway'.

A fashionable wedding group in the 1920s pose on the steps of the Parish Hall, Bude.

Morwenstow band, 1906. From left to right, back row: Dick Harris, Bert Burrow, Bill Cholwill, Archie Tape, Bill Oke, Harold Cholwill, Christie Cholwill. Front row: Lambert Cholwill, Fred Tape, John Cholwill, Claude Tape, Jack Oke.

A charabanc outing for Jacobstow bell-ringers, *c.* 1930.

Lifeboat Day celebrations in Bude have always featured sports and games on the canal. Here, in 1907, a large crowd has gathered to enjoy the fun, much as they do today. August Bank Holiday Monday is traditionally Lifeboat Day.

A leisurely trip along the Bude canal in the 1920s.

Promoting local produce is nothing new. At this church fête held in the Vicarage grounds in 1912, prime fresh goods are on offer, shame about the spelling!

During the First World War Bude scouts collected eggs for wounded servicemen. The placards record their progress. This collection point is at Colwills Dairy in Queen Street.

Six

Accommodation and Tourism

Seen here in the 1920s is Trevigue farmhouse near Highcliff in St Gennys, now owned by the National Trust. It remains a working dairy farm which also offers accommodation, and boasts an award-winning restaurant.

This final chapter sums it all up. Bude with its railway became in the 1920s and 30s (the 'Golden Years') a successful leading West Country seaside resort standing entirely on its own in North Cornwall. Here we see the large number of hotels, boarding and guesthouses which sprang up to supply the needs of the influx of our annual visitors. Alongside this are some of the facilities that Bude and district had to offer. This particular area was, and indeed still is, a great place with lots of local history.

The Falcon Hotel dates back to the early 1800s – the Regency period. The tariff in 1920 states a hot bath in your bedroom cost 1 shilling but a cold bath was only 6 pence!

The Erdiston private hotel, in the early part of the twentieth century. After major redevelopment it is now a large block of flats.

Left: The original Globe Hotel, situated on the Strand, in the late 1800s. *Right*: The Globe Hotel, rebuilt in 1903. This card was posted in 1910 to an address in London, describing it as being close to the beach with grand coastal scenery and in a picturesque neighbourhood.

In 1950 the Summerleaze Hotel still retained its private house facade.

The Burn View Hotel in 1950. It overlooked the golf course and was within walking distance of the clubhouse and town centre. During theb Second World War these premises served as an Officers' Mess.

In Killerton Road, standing detached from the business centre of Bude, is St Margarets Hotel. This card carries a Christmas greeting dated 1908. In early years the premises was a girls school.

The Grenville Hotel, built in 1911, dominates the skyline of Bude. It was extended in 1929 by the addition of a large wing to the left. It is no longer a hotel but an outdoor activities centre for young people.

The Penarvor Hotel was once the private residence of Sir George Croydon Marks, the Liberal Member of Parliament for North Cornwall in the 1920s. Its elevated position above Crooklets Beach gives it uninterrupted views over Bude bay.

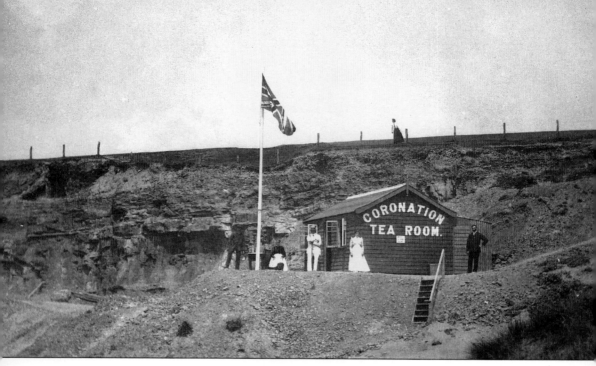

The impressively named Coronation Tea Room stands sentinel over Summerleaze Beach at the beginning of the twentieth century. The Coronation being that of Edward VII in 1902.

The largest hotel close to Crooklets Beach was the Hawarden Hotel, which was built in 1899 and named after the country home of Gladstone. The iron railings in the foreground which surrounded the golf course were removed in 1942 as war salvage.

The Westcliff Hotel, Bude. It was commandeered for military use in 1939, then between 1941 and 1945 it was home to Clifton College, evacuated from Bristol to escape the bombing.

The lounge of the Westcliff Hotel.

Efford Down House overlooking Summerleaze Beach, Bude, was built in 1875 by Arthur Mills, a director of the London & South Western Railway. It became a hotel in the 1930s and for many years was owned by the Workers Travel Association. It has now become residential apartments.

Set high above Coombe Valley was the manor house of Stowe, home of the Grenville family. All that remains now is the stable block, Stowe Barton, owned by the National Trust.

The Norfolk Hotel, situated in Lansdowne Road in the centre of Bude town, *c.* 1940. It was for many years a temperance hotel, but is now a business and retail premises.

The famous Tree Hotel, Stratton, *c.* 1930, home of Anthony Payne, the Cornish giant. Opposite is Rattenbury's hardware, jewellery and clockmakers shop, now demolished to provide a recreation area.

Situated beside the river Strat, the Bay Tree Hotel has long been a notable landmark when passing through Stratton.

Named after Sir Redvers Buller, a famous general in the Boer war, the Buller's Arms in Marhamchurch has provided a focal point for the village for many years.

This was the magnificent dining room of the Green Acres Hotel at Upton in the 1940s. It was renamed the Chough Hotel and latterly, Clements Restaurant and Hotel.

Rodds Bridge tea gardens were a refreshment stop for those enjoying boating on the canal in the 1940s.

To cater for the needs of an increasing number of tourists using Widemouth Bay Beach, these tea rooms and facilities were established by Mr W.J. Graver during the early 1920s.

An early caravanning holiday in Crackington Haven. The year is 1923.

Standing by the slipway to Crackington Beach is Penkenna House, complete with a gift shop, c. 1940. It was originally built as the stable block for the Coombe Barton.

A homely interior of the 1940s. This is the dining room of Penkenna House.

The Coombe Barton, a popular beach-side hotel and public house in Crackington Haven, seen here in the 1930s. It was built around 1750 for the 'captain' of the local slate quarry.

Halfway between Bude and Camelford, on the A39, stands the Wainhouse Corner Hotel and coaching stop. In the 1920s it was run by the Cory family.

The Bush Inn at Morwenstow, seen here in the 1920s, has managed to retain its character despite losing its thatched roof to a fire in 1968.

In the 1950s, with the increasing use of the private motor car for leisure, refreshment facilities sprang up at many beauty spots like this one at Sandymouth.

The quiet solitude of Coombe Valley tea gardens, *c.* 1940. A cream tea cost one shilling or a fruit tea including home-grown strawberries or raspberries in season would cost one and sixpence.

Penstowe Manor at Kilkhampton, home of the last true gentry in the area. Mrs Constance Thynne, who died at the age of ninety in 1961, was often seen being chauffeur driven around the area in her ancient Rolls Royce. She was a direct descendant of the Grenville family. The manor and grounds are now a holiday village.

124

The rock pools and wide expanse of sand at Summerleaze Beach, Bude, have long been a favourite spot for family outings. This picture was taken before the construction of the bathing pool.

Crooklets Beach, Bude, was originally called Maer ladies beach. Here in 1953 the first Surf Life Saving Club in Britain was formed.

These two readily identifiable features, known as Whaleback and Saddle rocks, represent the oldest tourist attraction Bude has to offer. The coastline attracts geologists from all over the world. This picture is from 1920 but any date could be substituted.

This picture of 1905 shows the old iron bridge which carried a narrow guage railway track onto Summerleaze Beach. Sand was transported from here to barges and carried inland by canal. In the background is Efford Cottage, one time home to members of the Acland family.

An aerial picture of Bude taken in 1920. Some easily located landmarks are Breakwater Road in the foreground, The Grenville Hotel, Central Methodist church and the Strand.

Belle Vue is today one of Bude's main shopping streets, but here in 1917 it was still residential properties.

It must be every author's prerogative to appear in his own book so I will exercise that right, here surrounded by other pupils of Miss Woodcock's class at Bude Primary School in 1958. From left to right, back row: Peter Luxton, Philip Rendell, Susan Walmsley, Ann Jennings, Pamela Barrett, Joan Bennett, Julie Tabb, -?-, Jackie Dredge, Anita Cotton, Roger Thorn. Middle row: Paul Jury, David Troke, Angela Laity, Peter Case, Brian Bennett, Adrian Abbott, Priscilla Bate, Philippa Gerry, Pat Ball, Jean Rainnie, Jane Vickery. Front row: Jenny Piedot, Roger Barlow, Janet Martindale, Jean Vodden, Diane Durston, Irene Couch, Pauline Ellacott, David Harris, -?-, Kenwyn Hooper, Paul Vickerstaff, Peter Selby.

Finally, a timeless scene from 1905 of swans on the Bude canal.